The Whispering Roots

C. DAY LEWIS

The Whispering Roots

JONATHAN CAPE
THIRTY BEDFORD SQUARE
LONDON

THIS COLLECTION FIRST PUBLISHED 1970
© 1970 BY C. DAY LEWIS

'The House where I was Born' first appeared in *Pegasus and Other Poems* (Jonathan Cape, 1957), and 'Fishguard to Rosslare' first appeared in *The Room and Other Poems* (Jonathan Cape, 1965).

JONATHAN CAPE LTD
30 BEDFORD SQUARE, LONDON WCI

SBN 224 61817 2

PRINTED AND BOUND IN GREAT BRITAIN
BY RICHARD CLAY (THE CHAUCER PRESS), LTD
BUNGAY, SUFFOLK

Contents

FOR SEAN AND ANNA

PART ONE

The House where I was Born

An elegant, shabby, white-washed house
With a slate roof. Two rows
Of tall sash windows. Below the porch, at the foot of
The steps, my father, posed
In his pony trap and round clerical hat.
This is all the photograph shows.

No one is left alive to tell me
In which of those rooms I was born,
Or what my mother could see, looking out one April
Morning, her agony done,
Or if there were pigeons to answer my cooings
From that tree to the left of the lawn.

Elegant house, how well you speak
For the one who fathered me there,
With your sanguine face, your moody provincial charm,
And that Anglo-Irish air
Of living beyond one's means to keep up
An era beyond repair.

Reticent house in the far Queen's County,
How much you leave unsaid.
Not a ghost of a hint appears at your placid windows
That she, so youthfully wed,
Who bore me, would move elsewhere very soon
And in four years be dead.

I know that we left you before my seedling
Memory could root and twine
Within you. Perhaps that is why so often I gaze
At your picture, and try to divine
Through it the buried treasure, the lost life—
Reclaim what was yours, and mine.

I put up the curtains for them again
And light a fire in their grate:
I bring the young father and mother to lean above me,
Ignorant, loving, complete:
I ask the questions I never could ask them
Until it was too late.

Ballintubbert House, Co. Laois

Here is the unremembered gate.
Two asses, a grey and a black,
Have ambled across from the rough lawn
As if they'd been told to greet
The revenant. Trees draw graciously back
As I follow the drive, to unveil
For this drifty wraith, composed and real
The house where he was born.

Nothing is changed from that sixty-year-old
Photograph, except
My father's young face has been brushed away.
On the steps down which he strolled
With me in his arms, the living are grouped,
And it is my son Sean
Who stands upon the dishevelled lawn
To photograph us today.

I walk through the unremembered house,
Note on the walls each stain
Of damp; then up the spacious stair
As if I would now retrace
My self to the room where it began.
Dust on fine furnishings,
A scent of wood ash – the whole house sings
With an elegiac air.

Its owner is not at home – nor I
Who have no title in it
And no drowned memories to chime
Through its hush. Can piety

Or a long-lost innocence explain it? —
By what prodigious spell,
Sad elegant house, you have made me feel
A ghost before my time?

Fishguard to Rosslare

From all my childhood voyages back to Ireland
Only two things remembered: gulls afloat
Off Fishguard quay, littering a patch of radiance
Shed by the midnight boat.

And at dawn a low, dun coast shaping to meet me,
An oyster sky opening above Rosslare ...
I rub the sleep from my eyes. Gulls pace the moving
Mast-head. We're almost there.

Gulls white as a dream on the pitch of Fishguard harbour,
Paper cut-outs, birds on a lacquered screen;
The low coastline and the pearl sky of Ireland;
A long sleep in between.

A sleep between two waking dreams – the haven,
The landfall – is how it appears now. The child's eye,
Unpuzzled, saw plain facts: I catch a glint from
The darkness they're haunted by.

Golden Age, Monart, Co. Wexford

There was a land of milk and honey.
Year by year the rectory garden grew
Like a prize bloom my height of summer.
Time was still as the lily ponds. I foreknew
No chance or change to stop me running
Barefoot for ever on the clover's dew.

Buttermilk brimmed in the cool earthen
Crocks. All day the french-horn phrase of doves
Dripped on my ear, a dulcet burden.
Gooseberry bushes, raspberry canes, like slaves
Presented myriad fruit to my mouth.
In a bliss of pure accepting the child moves.

Hand-to-mouth life at the top of the morning!
Shabby, queer-shaped house – look how your plain
Facts are remembered in gold engraving!
I have watched the dead – my simple-minded kin,
Once bound to a cramped enclave – returning
As myths of an Arcadian demesne.

Hens, beehives, dogs, an ass, the cobbled
Yard live on, brushed with a sunshine glaze.
Thanks to my gaunt, eccentric uncle,
His talkative sister, and the aunt who was
My second mother, from all time's perishable
Goods I was given these few to keep always.

Avoca, Co. Wicklow

Step down from the bridge.
A spit of grass points
At the confluence.

Tree he sat beneath
Spoiled for souvenirs,
Looks numb as driftwood.

A pretty fellow
In stone broods over
The meeting waters.

His words came alive
But to music's flow,
Like weeds in water.

I recall my aunt, my second mother,
Singing Tom Moore at the old rectory
Harmonium – *The Last Rose of Summer*,
She is far from the Land – her contralto
Scoop, the breathy organ, an oil lamp lit.
Words and tune met, flowed together in one
Melodious river. I drift calmly
Between its banks. Sweet vale of Avoca,
She is still young, I a child, and our two
Hearts like thy waters are mingled in peace.

Dublin tradesman's son,
Byron's friend, the pet
Of Whig drawing-rooms.

Fêted everywhere,
Everywhere at home,
He sang of exile

And death, tailoring
Country airs to a
Modish elegance.

Let the waters jig
In a light glitter,
So the source run full.

Near Ballyconneely, Co. Galway

i

A stony stretch. Grey boulders
Half-buried in furze and heather,
Purple and gold – Connemara's
Old bones dressed in colours
Out of a royal past.

Inshore the sea is marbled
And veined with foam. The Twelve Pins
Like thunderclouds hewn from rock
Or gods in a cloudy fable
Loom through an overcast.

The roofless dwellings have grown
Back to the earth they were raised from,
And tune with those primordial
Outcrops of grey stone
Among the furze and the heather.

Where man is dispossessed
Silence fills up his place
Fast as a racing tide.
Little survives of our West
But stone and the moody weather.

ii

Taciturn rocks, the whisht of the Atlantic
The sea-thrift mute above a corpse-white strand
Pray silence for those vanished generations
Who toiled on a hard sea, a harsher land.

Not all the bards harping on ancient wrong
Were half as eloquent as the silence here
Which amplifies the ghostly lamentations
And draws a hundred-year-old footfall near.

Preyed on by gombeen men, expropriated
By absentee landlords, driven overseas
Or to mass-burial pits in the great famines,
They left a waste which tourists may call peace.

The living plod to Mass, or gather seaweed
For pigmy fields hacked out from heath and furze—
No eye to spare for the charmed tourist's view,
No ear to heed the plaint of ancestors.

Winds have rubbed salt into the ruinous homes
Where turf-fires glowed once: waves and seagulls keen
Those mortal wounds. The landscape's an heroic
Skeleton time's beaked agents have picked clean.

Land

The boundary stone,
The balk, fence or hedge
Says on one side 'I own',
On the other 'I acknowledge'.

The small farmer carved
His children rations.
He died. The heart was halved,
Quartered, fragmented, apportioned:

To the sons, a share
Of what he'd clung to
By nature, plod and care—
His land, his antique land-hunger.

Many years he ruled,
Many a year sons
Followed him to oat-field,
Pasture, bog, down shaded boreens.

Turf, milk, harvest – he
Grew from earth also
His own identity
Firmed by the seasons' come-and-go.

Now at last the sons,
Captive though long-fledged,
Own what they envied once—
Right men, the neighbours acknowledge.

Kilmainham Jail: Easter Sunday, 1966

Sunbursts over this execution yard
    Mitigate high, harsh walls. A lowly
Black cross marks the deaths we are here to honour,
    Relieved by an Easter lily.
Wearing the nineteen-sixteen medal, a few
    Veterans and white-haired women recall
The Post Office, Clanwilliam House, the College of Surgeons,
    Jacob's factory – all
Those desperate strongholds caught in a crossfire
    Between the English guns
And Dublin's withering incredulity.
    Against the wall where once
Connolly, strapped to a chair, was shot, a platform
    Holds movie cameras. They sight
On the guard of honour beneath the tricolor,
    An officer with a horseman's light
And quiet hands, and now the old President
    Who, soldierly still in bearing,
Steps out to lay a wreath under the plaque.
    As then, no grandiose words, no cheering—
Only a pause in the splatter of Dublin talk,
    A whisper of phantom volleys.

How could they know, those men in the sunless cells,
What would flower from their blood and England's follies?
Their dreams, coming full circle, had punctured upon
The violence that gave them breath and cut them loose.
They bargained on death: death came to keep the bargain.
Pious postcards of men dying in spruce
Green uniforms, angels beckoning them aloft,
Only cheapen their cause. Today they are hailed
As martyrs; but then they bore the ridiculed shame of
Mountebanks in a tragedy which has failed.

And they were neither the one nor the other – simply
Devoted men who, though the odds were stacked
Against them, believed their country's age-old plight
And the moment gave no option but to act.
Now the leaders, each in his sweating cell,
The future a blind wall and the unwinking
Eyes of firing-squad rifles, pass their time
In letters home, in prayer. Maybe they are thinking
Of Mount Street, the blazing rooftops, the Post Office,
Wrapping that glory round them against the cold
Shadow of death. Who knows the pull and recoil of
A doomed heart?

         They are gone as a tale that is told,
The fourteen men. Let them be more than a legend:
Ghost-voices of Kilmainham, claim your due—
This is not yet the Ireland we fought for.
You living, make our Easter dreams come true.

Remembering Con Markievicz

Child running wild in woods of Lissadell:
Young lady from the Big House, seen
In a flowered dress, gathering wild flowers: Ascendancy queen
Of hunts, house-parties, practical jokes – who could foretell
(Oh fiery shade, impetuous bone)
Where all was regular, self-sufficient, gay
Their lovely hoyden lost in a nation's heroine?
Laughterless now the sweet demesne,
And the gaunt house looks blank on Sligo Bay
A nest decayed, an eagle flown.

The Paris studio, your playboy Count
Were not enough, nor Castle splendour
And fame of horsemanship. You were the tinder
Waiting a match, a runner tuned for the pistol's sound,
Impatient shade, long-suffering bone.
In a Balally cottage you found a store
Of Sinn Fein papers. You read – maybe the old sheets can while
The time. The flash lights up a whole
Ireland which you have never known before,
A nest betrayed, its eagles gone.

The road to Connolly and Stephen's Green
Showed clear. The great heart which defied
Irish prejudice, English snipers, died
A little not to have shared a grave with the fourteen.
Oh fiery shade, intransigent bone!
And when the Treaty emptied the British jails,
A haggard woman returned and Dublin went wild to greet her.
But still it was not enough: an iota
Of compromise, she cried, and the Cause fails.
Nest disarrayed, eagles undone.

Fanatic, bad actress, figure of fun—
She was called each. Ever she dreamed,
Fought, suffered for a losing side, it seemed
(The side which always at last is seen to have won),
Oh fiery shade and unvexed bone.
Remember a heart impulsive, gay and tender,
Still to an ideal Ireland and its real poor alive.
When she died in a pauper bed, in love
All the poor of Dublin rose to lament her
A nest is made, an eagle flown.

Lament for Michael Collins

Bicycling round Dublin with the ruddy, anonymous face
 Of a rural bank clerk, a price-tag on his head,
While a pack of Auxiliaries, informers, Castle spies,
 Nosing through snug and lodging, bayed
For the quarry that came and went like a shadow beneath its
 nose —

That was the Big Fellow, the schoolboy Pimpernel.
 Toujours l'audace, steel nerves and narrow shaves,
He loved to wrestle with comrades, he blubbered when they fell.
 Homeric heroes thus behaved:
He kept the form. But there's much more of the tale to tell.

With traitor and trigger-happy Tan he settled accounts.
 A martinet for balancing books, he slated
Unready reckoners, looked for no bonuses from chance,
 The risks he took being calculated
As a guerilla leader and an adept of finance.

They brought a Treaty. Now came the need to coax or drag
 His countrymen to some assured foothold
On the future out of their bitter and atavistic bog.
 Split was the nation he would build
And all to do again when the Civil War broke.

Fanaticism and muddle, Ireland wore down his heart
 Long before the ambush in County Cork,
Long before a random, maybe a treacherous shot
 Stopped it for ever. Do we talk
Of best-forgotten things and an elusive shade?

This country boy grown into a General's uniform,
 Gauntleted hands clasped in determination:

Tempestuous, moody man with the lashing tongue and the warm
       Sunbursts of laughter – dare a nation
Forget the genius who rode through storm on storm

To give it birth? You flying columns of ragtag cloud
     Stream from the west and weep over the grave
Of him who once dynamic as a powerhouse stood.
       For Ireland all he was he gave—
Energy, vision, last of all the great heart's blood.

Ass in Retirement

Ass
orbits
a firm stake:
each circle round
the last one is stamped
slow and unmomentous
like a tree-trunk's annual rings.

He does not fancy himself as a tragedian,
a circumference mystic or a treadmill hero,
nor takes he pride in his grey humility.
He is just one more Irish ass
eating his way round the clock,
keeping pace with his own appetite.

Put out to grass, given a yard more rope
each week, he takes time off from what's under his nose
only to bray at rain-clouds over the distant bog;
relishes asinine freedom – having to bear
no topple of hay, nor cleeves crammed with turf;
ignorant that he'll come in time

to the longest tether's end,
then strangle or accept
that stake. Either way
on the endless
grass one day
he'll drop
dead.

Beauty Show, Clifden, Co. Galway

They're come to town from each dot on the compass, they're
Wild as tinkers and groomed to an eyelash,
And light of foot as a champion featherweight
Prance on the top of the morning.

They walk the ring, so glossy and delicate
Each you'd think was a porcelain masterpiece
Come to life at the touch of a raindrop,
Tossing its mane and its halter.

The shy, the bold, the demure and the whinnier,
Grey, black, piebald, roans, palominos
Parade their charms for the tweedy, the quite un-
Susceptible hearts of the judges.

Now and again at the flick of an instinct,
As if they'd take off like a fieldful of rooks, they will
Fidget and fret for the pasture they know, and
The devil take all this competing.

The light is going, the porter is flowing,
The field a ruin of paper and straw.
Step neatly home now, unprized or rosetted,
You proud Connemara ponies.

Harebells over Mannin Bay

Half moon of moon-pale sand.
Sea stirs in midnight blue.
Looking across to the Twelve Pins
The singular harebells stand.

The sky's all azure. Eye
To eye with them upon
Cropped grass, I note the harebells give
Faint echoes of the sky.

For such a Lilliput host
To pit their colours against
Peacock of sea and mountain seems
Impertinence at least.

These summer commonplaces,
Seen close enough, confound
A league of brilliant waves, and dance
On the grave mountain faces.

Harebells, keep your arresting
Pose by the strand. I like
These gestures of the ephemeral
Against the everlasting.

At Old Head, Co. Mayo

In a fisherman's hat and a macintosh
He potters along the hotel drive;
Croagh Patrick is far beyond him now the locust
Has stripped his years of green.
Midges like clouds of memory nag
The drooped head. Fish are rising
Under his hat. He stops against the view.

All is a brushwork vision, a wash
Of new-laid colour. They come alive—
Fuchsia, grass, rock. The mist, which had unfocused
Mountain and bay, is clean
Forgot, and gone the lumpish sag
Of cloud epitomizing
Our ennui. Storms have blown the sky to blue.

He stops, but less to admire the view
Than to catch breath maybe. Pure gold,
Emerald, violet, ultramarine are blazing
From earth and sea: out there
Croagh Patrick stands uncapped for him.
The old man, shuffling by,
Recalls a rod lost, a dead girl's caress.

Can youthful ecstasies renew
Themselves in blood that has blown so cold?
Nature's more merciful: gently unloosing
His hold upon each care
And human tie, her fingers dim
All lights which held his eye,
And ease him on the last lap to nothingness.

Sailing from Cleggan

Never will I forget it—
Beating out through Cleggan Bay
Towards Inishbofin, how
The shadow lay between us,
An invisible shadow
All but severing us lay
Athwart the Galway hooker.

Sea-room won, turning to port
Round Rossadillisk Point I
Slacken the sheet. Atlantic
Breeze abeam, ahead sun's eye
Opening, we skirt past reefs
And islands – Friar, Cruagh,
Orney, Eeshal, Inishturk.

Porpoises cartwheeling through
Inshore water, boom creaking,
Spray asperging; and sunlight
Transforming to a lime-green
Laughter the lipcurling of
Each morose wave as they burst
On reefs fanged for a shipwreck.

Miracle sun, dispelling
That worst shadow! Salt and sun,
Our wounds' cautery! And how,
Havened, healed, oh lightened of
The shadow, we stepped ashore
On to our recaptured love—
Never could I forget it.

Ballintubber Abbey, Co. Mayo

'The Abbey that refused to die'

At the head of Lough Carra the royal abbey stands
Huge as two tithe-barns: much immortal grain
In its safe keeping, you might say, is stored.
Masons and carpenters have roofed and floored
That shell wherein a church not built with hands
For seven hundred and fifty years had grown.

I dare not quite say we were led here, driving
Through drifts of clobbering rainstorm (my own natal
Ballintubber is half Ireland away).
Yet, greeted by those walls of peregrine grey,
It felt like something more than the mere arriving
Of two sight-seers. Call it a destination.

Founded (1216) by Cathal O'Conor,
King of Connacht, the holy place was sacked by
Cromwellian louts, starved by the Penal Laws;
Yet all these troubled years, without a pause,
The Mass upheld God's glory, to the honour
Of Irishmen. So much for guidebook fact.

* * *

A seventeenth century crucifix, austere
Stonework will take the eye: the heart conceives
In the pure light from wall to whitewashed wall
An unseen presence, formed by the faith of all
The dead who age to age had worshipped here,
Kneeling on grass along the roofless nave.

And what is faith? The man who walks a high wire,
Eyes fixed ahead, believing that strong nets
Are spread below – the Hands which will sustain
Each fall and nerve him to climb up again.
Surefoot or stumbler, veteran or tiro,
It could be we are all God's acrobats.

Broaden that high wire now into a bridge
Where Christian men still meet over the fell
Abyss, and walk together: they should cling
Brothers in faith, not wranglers arguing
Each step and slip of the way. Such true religion
Renew this abbey of St Patrick's well!

Up-end the bridge. It makes a ladder now
Between mankind and the timeless, limitless Presence,
Angels ascending or descending it
On His quick errands. See this ladder's foot
Firm-planted here, where men murmur and bow
Like the Lough Carra reed-beds in obeisance.

An Ancestor

Seen once on a family tree, now lost,
Jane Eyre, of Eyrescourt, County Galway.
All I get from the name is a passionate
Prudish lady, crossed
In love, then happy-ended. Jane,
My Jane – while a boy called Patrick Prunty
Dug potatoes in County Down—
Lived upon her demesne.

No governess, an heiress she.
Well, knowing nothing of her – not even
The road to razed or shuttered Eyrescourt—
Like Charlotte I am free
To create a Jane. I give her a score
Of rowdy brothers and sisters, a hunting
Father, a gossipy mother, routs,
Flirtings and flames galore.

Pedigree mares, harp, scandal, new
Recipes fill the hours. I see her
Flitting towards an unclouded future
Down a damp avenue.
Were she alive, I know what would please
Her still – the traditional Anglo-Irish
Pastime of playing hide-and-seek
Among their family trees.

Goldsmith outside Trinity

There he stands, my ancestor, back turned
On Trinity, with his friend Edmund Burke
And others of the Anglo-Irish genius—
Poet, naturalist, historian, hack.

The statue glosses over his uncouth figure,
The pock-marked face, the clownish tongue and mien:
It can say nothing of his unstaunchable charity,
But does full justice to the lack of chin.

Little esteemed by the grave and grey-faced college,
He fiddled his way through Europe, was enrolled
Among the London literates: a deserted
Village brought forth a citizen of the world.

His period and the Anglo-Irish reticence
Kept sentiment unsicklied and unfurred:
Good sense, plain style, a moralist could distinguish
Fine shades from the ignoble to the absurd.

Dublin they flew, the wild geese of Irish culture.
They fly it still: the curdled elegance,
The dirt, the cod, new hucksters, old heroics,
Look better viewed from a remoter stance.

Here from his shadow I note the buses grumbling
On to Rathmines, Stillorgan, Terenure—
Names he'd have known – and think of the arterial
Through-way between us. I would like to be sure

Long-distance genes do more than merely connect us.
But I, a provincial too, an expatriate son
Of Ireland, have nothing of that compulsive gambler,
Nothing of the inspired simpleton.

Yet, as if to an heirloom given a child and long
Unvalued, I at last have returned to him
With gratefuller recognition, get from his shadow
A wordless welcome, a sense of being brought home.

The Whispering Roots

Roots are for holding on, and holding dear.
Mine, like a child's milk teeth, came gently away
From Ireland at the close of my second year.
Is it second childhood now – that I overhear
Them whisper across a lifetime as if from yesterday?

We have had blood enough and talk of blood,
These sixty years. Exiles are two a penny
And race a rancid word; a meaningless word
For the Anglo-Irish: a flighty cuckoo brood
Foisted on alien nests, they knew much pride and many

Falls. But still my roots go whispering on
Like rain on a soft day. Whatever lies
Beneath their cadence I could not disown:
An Irish stranger's voice, its tang and tone,
Recalls a family language I thrill to recognize.

All the melodious places only seen
On a schoolboy's map – Kinsale, Meath, Connemara:
Writers – Swift, Berkeley, Goldsmith, Sheridan:
Fighters, from Vinegar Hill to Stephen's Green:
The Sidhe, saints, scholars, rakes of Mallow, kings of Tara: –

Were background music to my ignorant youth.
Now on a rising wind louder it swells
From the lonely hills of Laois. What can a birth-
Place mean, its features comely or uncouth,
To a long-rootless man? Yet still the place compels.

We Anglo-Irish and the memory of us
Are thinning out. Bad landlords some, some good,
But never of a land rightfully ours,

We hunted, fished, swore by our ancestors,
Till we were ripped like parasite growth from native wood.

And still the land compels me; not ancestral
Ghosts, nor regret for childhood's fabled charms,
But a rare peacefulness, consoling, festal,
As if the old religion we oppressed all
Those years folded the stray within a father's arms.

The modern age has passed this island by
And it's the peace of death her revenants find?
Harsh Dublin wit, peasant vivacity
Are here to give your shallow claims the lie.
Perhaps in such soil only the heart's long roots will bind—

Even, transplanted, quiveringly respond
To their first parent earth. Here God is taken
For granted, time like a well-tutored hound
Brought to man's heel, and ghosting underground
Something flows to the exile from what has been forsaken.

In age, body swept on, mind crawls upstream
Toward the source; not thinking to find there
Visions or fairy gold – what old men dream
Is pure restatement of the original theme,
A sense of rootedness, a source held near and dear.

PART TWO

Some Beautiful Morning

'One can't tell whether there won't be a tide to catch, some beautiful morning.'

T. H. White

Yes, for the young these expectations charm
There are sealed sailing-orders; but they dream
A cabined breath into the favouring breeze
Kisses a moveless hull alive, will bear
It on to some landfall, no matter where—
The Golden Gate or the Hesperides.

Anchored, they feel the ground-swell of an ocean
Stirring their topmasts with the old illusion
That a horizon can be reached. In pride
Unregimentable as a cross-sea
Lightly they float on pure expectancy.
Some morning now we sail upon the tide.

Wharves, cranes, the lighthouse in a sleep-haze glide
Past them, the landmark spires of home recede,
Glittering waves look like a diadem.
The winds are willing, and the deep is ours
Who chose the very time to weigh the bowers.
How could they know it was the tide caught them?

* * *

Older, they wake one dawn and are appalled,
Rusting in estuary or safely shoaled,
By the impression made on those deep waters.
What most sustained has left a residue
Of cartons, peelings, all such galley spew,
And great loves shrunk to half-submerged french letters.

Sometimes they doubt if ever they left this harbour.
Squalls, calms, the withering wake, frayed ropes and dapper
Refits have thinned back to a dream, dispersed
Like a Spice Island's breath. Who largely tramped
The oceans, to a rotting hulk they're cramped—
Nothing to show for this long toil but waste.

It will come soon – one more spring tide to lift
Us off; the lighthouse and the spire shall drift
Vaguely astern, while distant hammering dies on
The ear. Fortunate they who now can read
Their sailing orders as a firm *God-speed,*
This voyage reaches you beyond the horizon

A Skull Picked Clean

Blank walls, dead grates, obliterated pages—
Vacancy filled up the house.
Nothing remains of the outward shows,
The inner rages.

Picture collection, trophies, library—
All that entranced, endorsed, enslaved—
With gimcrack ornaments have achieved
Nonentity.

How can I even know what it held most precious,
Its meaning lost, its love consumed?
Silence now where the cool brain hummed:
Where fire was, ashes.

How neatly those rough-tongued removal men
Have done the job. This useless key
They left us when they had earned their pay—
A skull, picked clean.

All Souls' Night

A hairy ghost, sent packing or appeased
    By dances, drums, and troughs of gore.
    A suave but fleshless ancestor
Honoured with fireworks at the birthday feast.

Safe in a harped and houried paradise:
    Pitchforked to some exemplary hell:
    Trooping through fields of asphodel:
Returned to nature's stock in a new guise—

For the cool corpse, impassive in its shroud,
    Such goings-on we have conceived.
    Born to injustice we believed
That underground or above the parting cloud

Pure justice reigns ... Seraphs may bear a wreath
    Past the unseeing mourner: he
    In euphemism and ceremony
Buries awhile the body of his own death.

*   *   *

All Souls' Night. Soon closing time will clear
A space for silence, last cars climb towards Kent
Throbbing like wind-torn snatches of lament.
Où sont des morts les phrases familières?

And where the dead? Like sun-warmed stones they keep
A little while their touch upon the living,
Remind us of their giving and forgiving,
Then, their fingers loosening, they sleep.

All that uneloquent congress of the shade
Speak through our truisms only, or they're crass
And mutinous like children in disgrace:
In clear or code no signal is relayed.

Who can know death, till he has dared to shave
His own corpse, rubbed his nose in his own noisome
Decay? Oh sweet breath, dancing minds and lissome
Bodies I've met with journeying to the grave!

It's they I want beside me – lovers, friends,
Prospective ghosts; not wind-blown atomies,
Dismantled bones, dissolving memories.
Tonight, a tingle of life at the nerve-ends.

*　*　*

But I may be the poorer for
    Not admitting souls
Into this human company:
    The dead have nothing else
For entrance-fee. Though bloodless, they
    Are brothers of the blood.
If they persist, how could I bar
    Such a convivial crowd?
Not willy-nilly thistledowns
    I fancy them, but as air
Viewless, dimensionless, pervasive,
    Here there and everywhere.
Born with souls, or soul-makers—
    Who knows? What I'm protesting
Is the idea that, if souls we have,
    They have to be everlasting.
I do not want an eternity
    Of self, rubbed clean or cluttered
With past. But it's unlikely that
    My wishes would be considered.

*　*　*

Welcome, all you intangible whose touch,
Impressing my own death upon my heart,
Leaves there a ghost of sweetness, like wood-ash
After the fires are out and the rooms aired.

To linger so, or as a horn that echoes
Out of the lost defiles, the sure defeat,
Heartening a few to courage and acceptance,
Is the short afterlife I'd want of fate.

Come then, dead friends, bringing your waft of wood-smoke,
Your gift of echoes. Sit by the bedside.
Graceless to ask just what I am invoking,
For this is the official visiting night.

Existences, consoling lies, or phantom
Dolls of tradition, enter into me.
Welcome, invisibles! We have this in common—
Whatever you are, I presently shall be.

Hero and Saint

Sad if no one provoked us any more
  To do the improbable—
Catch a winged horse, muck out a preposterous stable,
  Or even some unsensational chore

Like becoming a saint. Those adversaries knew
  The form, to be sure: small use for one
Who after an hour of effort would throw down
  Cross, shovel or lassoo.

It gave more prestige to each prince of lies
  And his far-fetched ordeal
That an attested hero should just fail
  One little finger's breadth from the prize.

Setting for Heracles and Bellerophon
  Such tasks, they judged it a winning gamble,
Forgetting they lived in a world of myth where all
  Conclusions are foregone.

A saint knows patience alone will see him through
  Ordeals which lure, disfigure, numb:
And this (the heroes proved) can only come
  From a star kept in view.

But he forgoes the confidence, the hallowed
  Air of an antique hero:
He never will see himself but as a zero
  Following a One that gives it value.

Hero imagined himself in the constellations,
  Saint as a numbered grain of wheat.
Nowhere but in aspiring do they meet
  And discipline of patience.

He rose to a trial of wit and sinew, *he*
    To improbable heights of loving.
Both, it seems, might have been good for nothing
    Without a consummate adversary.

Sunday Afternoon

'It was like being a child again, listening and thinking of
something else and hearing the voices – endless, inevitable
and restful, like Sunday afternoon.'

Jean Rhys

An inch beyond my groping fingertips,
Lurking just round the corner of the eye.
Bouquet from an empty phial. A sensual ellipse
So it eludes – the quicksilver quarry.

I stretch my hands out to the farther shore,
Between, the fog of Lethe: no river – a mere thread
Bars me from the self I would re-explore:
Powerless I am to break it as the dead.

Yet a picture forms. Summer it must be. Sunlight
Fixes deck-chairs and grass in its motionless torrents.
The rest are shadows. I am the real: but I could run
To those familiar shades for reassurance.

Light slithers from leaf to leaf. Gossip of aspens.
Cool voices blow about, sprinkling the lawn.
Bells hum like a windrush chime of bees: a tolling hastens
Long-skirted loiterers to evensong.

Flowers nod themselves to sleep at last. I smell
Roses – or is it an Irish nursemaid's florin scent?
Gold afternoon rounds to a breast ... Ah well,
A picture came, though not the one I meant.

Make what you can of it, to recompense
For the real thing, the whole thing vanished beyond recall.
Gauge from a few chance-found and cherished fragments
The genius of the lost original.

A Privileged Moment

Released from hospital, only half alive still,
Cautiously feeling the way back into himself,
Propped up in bed like a guy, he presently ventured
A glance at the ornaments on his mantelshelf.

White, Wedgwood blue, dark lilac coloured or ruby—
Things, you could say, which had known their place and price,
Gleamed out at him with the urgency of angels
Eager for him to see through their disguise.

Slowly he turned his head. By gust-flung snatches
A shower announced itself on the windowpane:
He saw unquestioning, not even astonished,
Handfuls of diamonds sprung from a dazzling chain.

Gently at last the angels settled back now
Into mere ornaments, the unearthly sheen
And spill of diamond into familiar raindrops,
It was enough. He'd seen what he had seen.

A Picture by Renoir

Two stocky young girls in the foreground stoop
For a ball – red dress, white pinafore.
Toned with the sunburnt grass, two more
Follow in beige. That wayward troupe
Is the butterfly soul of summer.

Beyond them a stripe of azure-blue
Distance fades to the kind of sky
That calls for larks. In the blend of high
Colour and hazy line is a clue
To the heart of childhood summer.

So lively they are, I can all but see
Those halycon girls elude the frame
And fly off the picture, intent on their game
Wherever the ball may go, set free
Into eternal summer.

It does what pictures are meant to do—
Grasp a moment and throw it clear
Beyond the reach of time. Those four
Maidens will play for ever, true
To all our youthful summers.

A Tuscan Villa

(for Kathleen and Johannes)

We took to your villa on trust and sight unseen
As the journey's dreamed-of height; had guessed it
A jewel framed in silver, nested in May-time green,
How the real thing surpassed it!
From the loggia, mountain ranges are seen renewing
Their mystery in the haze: a wedge
Of hill solid with jostled trees, cypresses queueing
Like travellers on their verge:
And at my feet in a lather of silvery fleece
An olive grove silently breaking.
Only a cuckoo, a child's cry breaks on the sylvan peace
And only to reawaken
The charm of silence. A burbling from the spaces
Up there reminds us that too soon
Bearing a spray of forget-me-not, leaving few traces
Behind, we shall move on.
But wrong it is, yearning to recompose
Feature on feature, petal by petal,
A blurring Paradise, the spectre of a rose.
I think they come too late – all
Gifts but the moment's. If we are quick and catch them,
We shall not grudge to let them fly.
Others will sojourn here: it will enrich them
With a present for ear and eye—
Silence and nightingales; the grace and knowledge
Of friends; acacia, lemon flowers,
Lemony tulips; a vista genial with vine and olive.
Today, be glad it is ours.

Merry-go-round

Here is a gallant merry-go-round.
The children all, entranced or queasy,
Cling to saddlebows, crazily fancy the
Circular tour is a free and easy
Gallop into a world without end.
Now their undulating time is up.
Horses, music slow to a stop.

Time's last inches running out,
A vortex, only guessable
Before by the circus ring of bubbles
Sedately riding, now turns visible—
A hole, an ulcer, a waterspout.
Bubbles twirl faster as closer they come
To the brink of the vacuum.

And my thoughts revolve upon death's
Twisted attraction. As limbs move slower,
Time runs more quickly towards the undoer
Of all. I feel each day devour
My future. Still, to the lattermost breath
Let me rejoice in the world I was lent—
The rainbow bubbles, the dappled mount.

Philosophy Lectures

He goes about it and about,
By elegant indirections clears a route
To the inmost truth.
Cutting the ground from underneath
Rogue analogies, dialectic tares,
See how he bares
And shames the indulgent, weed-choked soil,
Shaving his field to the strictly meaningful!
Now breathless we
Await, await the epiphany—
A miracle crop to leap from the bald ground

Not one green shoot, however, is discerned.

Well, watch this reaper-and-binder bumbling round
A shuddered field. Proud sheaves collapse
In narrowing squares. A coarser job, perhaps—
Corn, corn cockle and poppy lie
Corded, inseparable. Now each eye
Fastens on that last stand of corn:
Hares, partridge? – no, surely a unicorn
Or phoenix will be harbouring there,
Ripe for revelation. Harvest forgot, I stare
From the field's verge as the last ears fall.

Not even a rabbit emerges. Nothing at all.

Are the two fields identical,
Only the reapers different? Misdirected
Or out of our minds, we expected
A wrong thing – the impossible
Or merely absurd; creatures of fire and fable
Where bread was the intention,

Harvest where harvest was not meant.
Yet in both fields we saw a right end furthered:
Something was gathered.

After an Encaenia

This afternoon the working sparrows, glum
Of plumage, nondescript, flurried, quarrelsome,
Appear as cardinal, kingfisher, hoopoe, bird
Of paradise. They stalk the sward

With gait somnambulous beside their not
So colourful hens, or heart to gorgeous heart
Absently confer together
In tones that do not change to match their feathers.

Will no one tell me what they chirp? I'd say
Their minds are very far away
From this cloud-cuckoo lawn, impatient to
Resume the drudgery sparrows pursue.

Scavengers are they? Gathering crumbs,
Nibbling at particles and old conundrums,
Pouncing on orts never observed before,
They justify their stay-at-home exploring.

I like these scrap-collectors: and to see
Their hard-earned plumes worn without vanity
Hints that a scholar's search for evidence
Is selfless as the lives of saints.

Truth, knowledge even, seems too grandiose
A word for the flair and flutterings of those
Whose ambition is no more wide
Than to get, once for all, one small thing right.

Tenure

is never for keeps, never truly assured
(tick on, you geological clocks)
though some things almost have it, or seem to have it.
For example, rocks
in a shivering sea: the castaway who has clawed himself on
to one:
a bull's tenacious horn:
archaic myths: the heroin habit.
Even the sun or a dead man's skull among the cactus
does not quite have it.

I turn now to American university practice.
Tenure there is pronounced 'Shangri-
La': once you have it, however spurious
your fame, not even the angriest
trustees, except for certified madness or moral turpitude,
can ever dislodge you. I salute
all those tenurious
professors. But I would not wish to be
one, though the life may be happy and sometimes not inglorious.

Tenure is not for me.
I want to be able to drop out of my head,
or off my rock and swim to another, ringed with a roundelay
of sirens. I should not care to be a dead
man's skull, or a myth, or a junkie:
or the too energetic sun.
Since heaven and earth, we are told, shall pass away
(hell, sneers the blonde, is off already)
I would live each day as if it were my last and first day.

Epitaph for a Drug-Addict

Mourn this young girl. Weep for society
Which gave her little to esteem but kicks.
Impatient of its code, cant, cruelty,
Indifference, she kicked against all pricks
But the dream-loaded hypodermic's. She
Has now obtained an everlasting fix.

A Marriage Song

(for Albert and Barbara)

Midsummer, time of golden views and hazes,
Advance in genial air,
Bring out your best for this charmed pair—
Let fly a flamingo dawn, throw open all your roses,
Crimson the day for them and start the dancing.

June-month fruits, yield up your delicate favours
Entrancing them, and be
Foretastes of ripe felicity:
Peach bloom and orange flower, ravish these happy lovers,
Sweeten the hour for them and start the dancing.

Tune to our joy, grass, breezes, philomels,
Enhancing their bright weather
Of inward blessedness; together
With honeying bees and silver waterfalls of bells
Carol our hopes for them, oh start the dancing.

In well-deep looks of love and soft-as-foam
Glances they plight their troth.
Midsummer stars, be kind to both
Through the warm dark when they shall come into their
    own,
Light your candles for them, start the dance.

At East Coker

At the far end of a bemusing village
Which has kept losing finding and losing itself
Along the lane, as if to exercise a pilgrim's
Faith, you see it at last. Blocked by a hill
The traffic, if there was any, must swerve aside:
Riding the hilltop, confidently saddled,
A serviceable English church.

Climb on foot now, past white lilac and
The alms-house terrace; beneath yew and cedar
Screening the red-roof blur of Yeovil; through
The peaceable aroma of June grasses,
The churchyard where old Eliots lie. Enter.

A brass on the south wall commemorates
William Dampier, son of this unhorizoned village,
Who thrice circumnavigated the globe, was
First of all Englishmen to explore
The coast of Australia ... An exact observer
Of all things in Earth, Sea and Air. Another
Exploring man has joined his company.

In the north-west corner, sealed, his ashes are
(Remember him at a party, diffident,
Or masking his fire behind an affable mien):
Above them, today, paeonies glow like bowls of
Wine held up to the blessing light.

Where an inscription bids us pray
For the repose of the soul of T. S. Eliot, poet—
A small fee in return for the new worlds
He opened us. 'Where prayer is valid', yes,
Though mine beats vainly against death's stone front,

And all our temporal tributes only scratch
Graffiti on its monumental silence.

*　　*　　*

But soon obituary yields
To the real spirit, livelier and more true.
There breathes a sweetness from his honoured stone,
A discipline of long virtue,
As in that farmside chapel among fields
At Little Gidding. We rejoice for one
Whose heart a midsummer's long winter,
Though ashen-skied and droughtful, could not harden
Against the melting of midwinter spring,
When the gate into the rose garden
Opening at last permitted him to enter
Where wise man becomes child, child plays at king.
A presence, playful yet austere,
Courteously stooping, slips into my mind
Like a most elegant allusion clinching
An argument. Eyes attentive, lined
Forehead – 'Thus and thus runs,' he makes it clear,
'The poet's rule. No slackening, no infringing
'Must compromise it.' ... Now, supplying
Our loss with words of comfort, his kind ghost
Says all that need be said about committedness:
Here in East Coker they have crossed
My heart again – For us there is only the trying
To learn to use words. The rest is not our business.